ECIDUJERP
PREJUDICE
ECIDUJERP
PREJUDICE
ECIDUJERP
PREJUDICE

*Either Way It
Doesn't Make Sense*

The Samuel Dalsimer Series

honors the late Samuel Dalsimer, New York, N.Y., who served as National Chairman of the Anti-Defamation League of B'nai B'rith. In sponsoring this series, the Anti-Defamation League commemorates the exemplary humanity and devotion to democratic principles which characterized and inspired Mr. Dalsimer's many years of service to the League.

ECIDUJERP
PREJUDICE

EITHER WAY IT DOESN'T MAKE SENSE

*By Irene Fandel Gersten
and Betsy Bliss*

*Illustrated by
Richard Rosenblum*

FRANKLIN WATTS | NEW YORK | LONDON

Library of Congress Cataloging in Publication Data

Gersten, Irene Fandel.
    Ecidujerp, prejudice.

    SUMMARY: Discusses the types of prejudice, their
causes and effects and methods of combating them.
        1. Prejudices and antipathies–Juvenile literature.
[1. Prejudices] I. Bliss, Betsy, 1942-   joint author.
II. Rosenblum, Richard, illus. III. Title.
BF575.P9G49   301.45   73-10371
ISBN 0-531-02669-8

This book was published in cooperation with the Anti-Defamation League of B'nai B'rith.

The authors gratefully acknowledge the editorial assistance of Carol Hymowitz and Nina B. Link.

CONTENTS

ECIDUJERP
PREJUDICE
ECIDUJERP
PREJUDICE
ECIDUJERP
PREJUDICE

*Either Way It
Doesn't Make Sense*

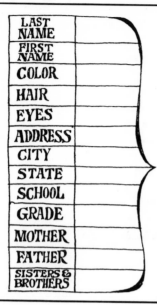

LAST NAME	
FIRST NAME	
COLOR	
HAIR	
EYES	
ADDRESS	
CITY	
STATE	
SCHOOL	
GRADE	
MOTHER	
FATHER	
SISTERS & BROTHERS	

1

PREJUDICE: PEOPLE OR GROUPS?

"Every Man Is In Some Ways
Like All Other Men,
Like Some Other Men,
Like No Other Man."
Clyde Kluckhohn

Who am I? It sounds like a simple question. Think about it for a minute and you will see that it is very difficult to answer.

When we are very young, we realize how similar we are to all the other people around us. Our faces and bodies are more alike than they are different. We all have the ability to think, talk, write, and solve problems. No one has ever mistaken a man for a rose, a tiger, or an eel. Human beings are a separate, very special group.

As we grow older, we learn to recognize some physical differences among people like skin and hair color, height and weight. There are also differences in the way we think and act. It is in discovering how different we are in so many ways and yet the same in so many ways that we can begin answering the question — Who am I?

We answer this question in a number of different ways with the passing of time. To young children, the question seems easy to answer. "I am Susan," "I am George," "I am Caroline." As we get older, we realize that we are part of a family unit, and we respond, "I am Susan Klein" (Susan, a member of the Klein family unit), "I am George Blue-Sky" (George, a member of the Blue-Sky family unit).

What we are is always changing because we are constantly growing and learning new things. For example, when we begin to spend a lot of our time in school, we discover that we have become "students." What this means is that we are part of a school unit as well as a family unit. It also means that more and more things will be expected of us. With the passing years, we become a part of more and more groups. In answering the question of who we are, it becomes easier and easier to describe ourselves in terms of the different groups to which we belong.

4

GROUPS | At some point we realize that people belong to one of the two sex groups, one of many racial types, and one of a number of religions. The amount of money you earn, your job, and your level of education all define other groups to which you will eventually belong. A high school graduate and a college graduate would be in different educational groups, just as a secretary and a doctor would be in different job groups. Susan, who as a child described herself simply as Susan, and then as Susan Klein, a member of the Klein family unit, now describes herself as Susan Klein, white, female, American, Jewish, upper middle class, and a lawyer. George has also developed a larger identity. He is now George Blue-Sky, red, male, American, Indian, Hopi, middle class, teacher.

These are just a few of the groups that people can fit themselves into. Take yourself, for example. How many groups would you fit into? Where would you start? With your age, your sex? What would you include? The color of your hair and eyes, the neighborhood you live in, the length of your hair, the kind of clothes you wear, the kind of car your father drives, your mother's job, the school your sister goes to?

All of these things tell a lot about what you are. They give some important facts about you, but which of these groups really describes the kind of person you are?

We know some things about Susan Klein and George Blue-Sky because we know some of the groups that they fit into. We know about them, but we don't know them as people. For example, we don't know if George is kind and has a sense of humor, or if Susan is friendly and considerate of other people. Nor do we really know you if we know what your mother's job is, what kind of car your father drives, what neighborhood you live in, or how you wear your hair.

To know you or Susan or George, rather than to know about

you, we must meet with you, talk to you, spend some time with you. If we think we know who you are because we know what your religion is, or what school your sister goes to, we are making a great mistake.

LABELING | Our minds take the things we learn and put them into groups by giving them labels or name tags. From childhood we learn to understand the world by putting similar things into a group. First we learn words like "milk" and "meat," and we put them into the "food" group, or words like "black," "white," and "yellow," and we put them into the "color" group.

There is nothing wrong with the way our minds sort things into groups. It allows us to store and remember a lot of information.

We often need to know about objects before we taste, smell, or touch them. We prejudge a lemon as sour without tasting it, just as we know that fire will burn without touching it. But when we prejudge all dogs as friendly, all fat people as jolly, or all cats as mean and nasty, we are making a broad general statement that is not true.

It is a mistake to try and group hair color, skin color, religion, and race with an individual's intelligence or personality. The fact that a lemon is yellow has nothing to do with its sourness, and we would be in error if we used the color yellow as a measure of sourness in other foods, such as corn.

We must remember that grouping things together can tell us something about an object or person, but it does not show us the whole picture. We know that "meat" is something that we can eat when we know that it fits into the "food" group. But we do not know if we will like it or dislike it, if we will think it something good or something bad. All that we will know about meat is that it is something we can eat.

PREJUDICE | It is very dangerous to have an opinion about a group and to judge all the people in that group according to that opinion. When we confuse the individual with the group in this way, we are guilty of prejudice.

Prejudice comes from the word "prejudge." We prejudge when we have an opinion about a person because we feel a certain way about the group to which he belongs.

For example, Susan Klein would be guilty of prejudice if she considered George Blue-Sky ignorant because she thought all Indians were ignorant. She would be guilty of prejudice because her opinion of George Blue-Sky would be based on a judgment formed before she met or even heard of George Blue-Sky.

Groups tell us only what a person or thing may be like. If we know that George Blue-Sky is an Indian, we know only that we can expect him to have a certain background and certain general kinds of experiences. We can't know any more about George because he is an Indian than we can know about "meat" because it is a "food." To know what kind of flavor "meat" has, we must taste it. To know what kind of person George is, we must meet him and talk with him.

An example of why it is important to react to people as individuals and not simply as members of a group was found in a recent study of white people in a neighborhood into which black people were moving. Many of the white people were unhappy that blacks were entering their neighborhood, and they said that they didn't want to be neighbors with blacks because blacks were "troublemakers." After some time had passed, another study was done and it was discovered that those white people who actually had new black neighbors no longer had bad feelings toward them. The white families living next door to the black families were forced to see these families as indi-

viduals — as mothers, fathers, sisters, brothers, aunts, uncles, and grandparents. They saw each other every day, doing the same tasks, leaving for work and school, going marketing, eating dinner. It was only those white residents who did not live really close to the black families who continued to feel prejudiced and were unhappy. They still saw those black individuals as a group.

Groups and labels don't deal with feelings. They give us only facts. When we add feeling to fact — that is, when we begin placing our personal opinions on groups of things and people — we are guilty of prejudice.

None of us fits into only one group. We are all, each and every one of us, capable of being many people. Because we are many people, we slip in and out of groups. The groups that we fit into show only a part of what we are. They do not show who we are.

If we are ever to answer the question of who we are, we must remember where our differences end and our similarity begins.

We are similar to each other because we are all human beings.

We are more like some people than other people because we share similar interests, goals, and backgrounds.

We are like no other person because each of us sees the world in a unique and very special way.

I knew a man who had lost the use of both eyes.
He was called a "blind man."
He could also be called a fine typist,
a hard worker, a good student,
a careful listener, a man who wanted a job.
But he couldn't get a job in the department store
order room where workers sat and
typed orders which came over the telephone.

The personnel man wanted to get
the interview over quickly.
"But you're a blind man," he kept saying.
And one could almost feel his silent thought
that somehow being blind made
the man unable to do anything.
So blinded by the label was the personnel man
that he would not look beyond it.
I.J. Lee

2

PREJUDICE: WHAT IS IT?

There is a certain illness within you
So there is a certain illness in me
And there is illness in this whole wide world
The illness is the lack of love.
Arleen Blackwell, Age 13

Prejudice has a long history. In some ways we haven't changed very much with the passing of time. For hundreds of years people have been judged by the groups they belong to rather than by who they are as individuals.

When the Normans conquered the Saxons in 1066, they passed many laws to separate themselves from the Saxons and even forbade them to use their own language in law courts and other important places. Four hundred years ago in Europe, thousands of people died in religious wars between Protestants and Catholics. Not very long ago in Russia and in Germany, millions of Jews were tortured, put behind bars, and killed, simply because they were Jews.

Our own country, America, was founded by people fleeing prejudice in England — people who did not belong to the "right group." Men and women from Ireland, Germany, and France came to our country in search of freedom and a new life. Oddly enough, many of the Americans already here treated the newcomers with the same prejudice that they themselves had once been victims of. The American Indian, the earliest American, became the victim of both of these groups of immigrants.

And the history we make today is still full of prejudice. In the last thirty years in this country, minority groups — groups that do not make up the major part of our country — have fought hard for equal rights under the law. Right now, Indians, women, blacks, and Mexican Americans, to name just a few, are still struggling to find a place within American society. Protestants and Catholics are still fighting one another in some parts of the world. In South Africa, whites forced black people to leave their homes and move to "blacks only" areas. In England, immigrants from India suffered a great deal of hardship because of the prejudice directed against them. For the past four years in Greece, it has been against the law for men to have long hair and for women to wear mini-skirts. In most countries of the world, women are treated unfairly simply because they are women and are thought not to be as good as men are.

RECOGNIZING PREJUDICE | Prejudice is not always easy to see. Most people deny that they are prejudiced, but they joke easily about people from different races or countries. Others try to avoid getting to know people they consider to be "different." Some don't want their neighbors to have a different color or different religion from theirs. They don't want to work or play with anyone who doesn't think about the world in the same way they do. They separate the world into "us" and "them," and they act as if they expect "others" to be "bad," "stupid," "dirty," or even "dangerous."

How do people show their prejudice? Sometimes they fight with those they do not like. Sometimes one group attacks an individual of another group. At other times two different groups fight. More often, however, people separate themselves from those they consider to be "others." They separate themselves in their schools, in their neighborhoods, and in the clubs they join.

An example of this kind of attitude can be found if we look at the way the Japanese were treated in this country around the turn of the century. Many Japanese came and settled on the west coast of the United States during the second half of the nineteenth century. They met with a great deal of prejudice because they looked so very different from most of the people in the towns they lived in. The people on the west coast wanted to separate themselves from these newcomers, and in 1906 the School Board of San Francisco barred all children of Japanese families from the public school system and created special schools for the Japanese students only. Although President Roosevelt made the school board change its mind the next year and admit Japanese pupils under sixteen years of age, he had to promise not to allow any more Japanese workers to enter this country in order to get the school board to keep its word.

What makes people seem "different" to one another is the fact that they don't fit into the same groups. "Others" are simply people who belong to groups that are different from yours. Isn't it strange that we all want to be considered special but that we will not give the same consideration to other people? We see ourselves as one of a kind, but we often will not allow people from other groups the right to be different from us.

The prejudice that the Chinese met with in the nineteenth and early twentieth centuries is a good example of how bad feelings develop because of simple physical and social differences. The Chinese arrived in America during the building of the great railroads. They obtained jobs at the railroad companies and did a great deal of work, laying tracks and clearing land. Without their help, the railroads certainly could not have been built as rapidly as they were. When the railroads were completed, the Chinese tried to find other kinds of work. But jobs were hard to get. People were angry at the Chinese because they thought they had taken jobs away from people who had been born here. The real problem was that the Chinese seemed so different. There was a strong physical difference because the Chinese people kept their national dress and the custom of wearing their hair in long braids. Because they looked so different, they became an easy target to spot. Gangs used to capture Chinese men and cut off their braids. The prejudice against the Chinese got worse and worse as the Chinese people kept trying to be themselves. Finally the American people just stopped the entrance of any Chinese into this country for a long time.

LEARNING PREJUDICE | How do people become prejudiced? Since everybody doesn't like something, is it natural to be prejudiced? Why are some people more prejudiced than others?

Just a hundred years ago, most people believed that we were born prejudiced. They thought prejudice was natural. Today we know that this is not true. Today we know that parents do not physically pass on prejudice to their children.

Today we know that we all learn to hate.

We learn from our parents, our friends, our teachers, classmates, neighbors, movies, television, books, newspapers — all of our surroundings. Sometimes we learn prejudice directly from other people. But most often nobody tells us exactly what kinds of things or people are "good" or "bad." Instead, we get the idea of what we should like and not like by the way people around us act.

One day a social worker found a little boy standing in the street crying. When she asked him what was wrong, he told her that he had been hit by a "Polish boy." Several of the people standing around said that the boy in question was not Polish at all, but the little boy insisted that he had been hit by a "Polish boy." This seemed so odd that the social worker tried to find out about the little boy's family. She found that he lived in the same apartment house with a Polish family. His Italian mother was always arguing with her Polish neighbor, and had put into the heads of her children the idea that "bad" and Polish were the same thing.

We use our own surroundings as a way of measuring what is good or what is bad, and most people tend to believe that their own surroundings and their own way of life are best. We all fear the unknown and the unfamiliar. We stay within our own groups because it is more comfortable. We know what to expect from the people in our own group and they know what to expect from us.

Scientists tell us that although prejudice is not a natural inborn reaction, fear of the unknown and unfamiliar is. From childhood, we would rather stay within the limits of what we know than explore new situations.

Remember how uneasy we all are on the first day of the new school year. We wonder what the year will bring us, what our new classmates will be like, and, of course, what kind of person our new teacher will be. This is just a small example of how we feel about the unknown.

A famous writer on child care pointed out recently that "babies are against everything that isn't Mother. It is up to Mother to get babies to accept the rest of the world."

As an example of this, imagine that you are a stranger entering a house for the first time to meet a mother and her new baby. What will the baby do when he sees you?

He will probably cry with fear. You are different. Your voice, your clothes, your face, your way of moving are different from any other person the baby knows. And so he is frightened. This is only natural. We are all afraid at first of strange things.

What the baby's mother does will make a big difference. Does she hold him close, to keep him away from the "different person"? Does she protect him, as if you are dangerous? Or does she welcome you, the stranger, with a smile, showing the baby that people who are unfamiliar may really be nice? Just a simple smile may have a lot to do with whether the baby grows up liking or not liking "different" people.

It is from a situation like this that we may begin to learn about prejudice. When we do not get to see people who are different from ourselves and our family, we are not given the chance to overcome our natural fear of the unfamiliar and unknown.

PREJUDICE AND IGNORANCE | Suppose that you had never met an old person. Suppose that your friends told you that "all old people are crazy." Would you believe them? You might — if you had never known an old person. That is what happens when we insist on knowing only people just like ourselves.

This kind of prejudice is really *ignorant* prejudice — prejudice due to not knowing better. It is expressed by many people who keep themselves separate and do not mix with other groups.

Ignorant prejudice was what those white residents felt when the black families began to move into their neighborhood. But when they were actually living next door to one another, they started to look at their black neighbors as individuals and to see that they were not noisy or troublemakers, but were honest, warm, hardworking people, very much like themselves.

REAL PREJUDICE | It is important to remember that there is a difference between ignorance and prejudice. Ignorance means forming an opinion without really knowing the facts. The prejudice that often results from ignorance does not necessarily mean hateful feelings.

Real prejudice, on the other hand, occurs when we choose to keep bad opinions even when we have a chance to know better. Prejudice occurs when a person refuses to change his mind — even when the facts show him that he is wrong.

Mark is an example of a person with real prejudice.

When Mark was young, all of his friends and classmates told him that all black people were "lazy" and "dirty." Mark took their word for it.

He believed them because he had never seen a person with dark skin. There were no black people in his school, his neighborhood, or his Boy Scout troop. When he went to the movies, he hardly ever saw black people in films. Those that he did see were shown as "lazy" and "dirty." The same was true on television. Mark was a very protected person who had little touch with the world outside of his own group.

As Mark grew older and left his neighborhood, he began to see some people with dark skin. But they seemed so different from him. They looked different. They dressed differently and they even talked differently. Mark stayed away from them because they were strange and he was afraid of them. Mark covered his fear by saying that "they" were "dirty" and "lazy."

When Mark entered high school, he met Jeff, who was black. Jeff was in most of his classes and Mark was forced to see that Jeff was neat, well-dressed, and very hardworking. But Mark refused to change his bad opinions of all dark-skinned people. Even though he knew Jeff to be much like himself, his prejudice would not allow him to see Jeff as a complete individual. Mark could not see beyond Jeff's dark skin. He said to himself, "Jeff is different from other blacks. It is still true that all those people are 'dirty and lazy.'" Mark simply could not see that "all those people" are individuals just like Jeff.

PREJUDICE AND PROFIT | Why do Mark and people like him refuse to give up their prejudices even when the facts show them to be wrong? Why do people prejudge others in the first place? Why has man, for as long as we can remember, been cruel to his fellow man? Why is prejudice as much a problem today as it was four hundred years ago?

To answer these questions isn't easy. Mostly, we act in a prejudiced manner because we expect to gain something.

Each individual is a complex being, with many different needs, desires, and goals. And though people are guilty of prejudice because they believe they will gain something, what it is that they want to gain is different in almost every case.

The history of the treatment of the American Indian is full of instances of prejudice caused by the desire for profit. The main reason for conflict between the Indians and the white settlers was land. The whites wanted more and more land, and to get it, they had to take it away from the Indians. When there was no more land available to the white man east of the Mississippi, he became greedy for the rich land that was held by the Indians. President Andrew Jackson had been active in earlier wars against the Indians and he did not like them very much. President Jackson went against a decree by Judge John Marshall of the Supreme Court and permitted the white settlers to try to take the land from the Indians. President Jackson tried to solve the problem by promising the Indians land farther west, but he soon took that away from them, too. Finally, the Indians lost everything they had. The white people wanted the land of the Indians and so they convinced themselves that the Indians were "savages" and not as good as white men. They wanted to believe this so that they wouldn't feel bad about stealing the land of the Indians.

CONFORMING PREJUDICE | A very common type of prejudice comes from our need to have the same values as the group to which we belong. We tend to feel safe within our own group. It makes us feel important. To know we will be accepted by that group, we adopt the group's thinking. When the group thinking is prejudiced, we often accept this thinking because we are afraid to go against the group.

A college student recently wrote about an example of this kind of prejudice. It occurred on his first day of high school. He had been talking with a boy of his own age when one of the older students came over to him and said, "Don't you know that Harry is a Jew?" He had never before met a Jew and really didn't care whether or not Harry, whom he had started to like, was a Jew. But he admitted that the tone of the older boy's voice was enough to convince him that he had better not make Harry his friend.

When we act in this way, we are clearly in the wrong. There is nothing wrong in wanting to belong to a certain group because we want to feel a part of something. We all need friends and want to feel safe and needed. But there is something terribly wrong when we become a part of the group and are no longer an individual. By giving up what is special in each of us, we can no longer act or think on our own. We become a group body. We are afraid to make a step on our own two feet. We act in a prejudiced way not because we believe the others are not as good as we are, but because we are afraid of being "different" and of having opinions different from those of our friends, classmates, and family.

SCAPEGOATING | There is one kind of prejudice that occurs when we want to go along with the opinions of our friends. There is a more dangerous kind of prejudice that stems from feeling unsure about ourselves and from the questions we have about our own worth as individuals. It is called scapegoating.

It is part of human nature for people to compare themselves with one another. It is part of our society for individuals to

compete with one another for money and personal rewards. Often our feeling of being not as good, as attractive, as wealthy, as skilled, or as successful as others makes us need to blame someone else for our own shortcomings.

It is difficult for people to accept their own weaknesses. It is much easier to blame our problems on others. When we look down on someone else, we seem so much taller.

The word "scapegoating" comes from Biblical times. Then a scapegoat was let loose in the wilderness after the high priest had placed the sins of the people on its head. All of the failures, the shortcomings, and the shameful things that the people were guilty of were put onto the goat. Sending the goat out into the woods was the people's way of separating themselves from their guilt. They were no longer responsible for their own actions. Today we use the word scapegoat to describe a person or a group of people who are blamed unfairly.

Scapegoating is in many ways like labeling. Both are lazy ways of thinking. Both can prevent a person from seeing himself as he really is. When we put people into groups, we hide ourselves or other people behind name tags. We see only a part of what people really are, not the whole picture.

Our world is full of people like Mr. Jones.

Mr. Jones is very upset about what is happening in this country. Mr. Jones says, "The reason we have riots is that there are outsiders in this country." He adds, "If we could only get rid of the outsiders, everything would be fine."

Riots, like most problems, have many causes. Solutions are hard to find and Mr. Jones doesn't want to bother to find out what all of the causes are. It is much easier to find someone to blame, to find a scapegoat. For Mr. Jones, "outsiders" are handy scapegoats.

It is usually easy to recognize the Mr. Joneses of the world. They are the people who can say, "If only we didn't have so-and-so, everything would be okay." These persons will find one enemy to explain everything that is wrong. "If only we didn't have Jews —" or "If only we didn't have hippies —."

But nothing is that simple.

Prejudiced people who scapegoat say the same things about all groups that are different from their own. No matter who the prejudiced person is blaming, that "enemy" is "lazy" and "dirty" and "dangerous". The prejudiced person warns everyone against "marrying those people" or "getting close to those people" or "believing anything those people say." You can substitute almost any kind of human being for "those people," but the prejudiced person's remarks and warnings will be the same.

That is because the scapegoater does not hate any one person in particular. He hates a "group that is different," and his hatred covers all the members of that group.

DEFENDING PREJUDICE | When people say the kinds of things that Mark, for example, said about Jeff, they do not always know that they are guilty of prejudice. Most prejudiced people try to hide their true fears from themselves as well as from others. These people feel good only when they believe that there are others who are not quite as good as they are.

Practically nobody will admit to being prejudiced. Practically everybody agrees that prejudice is cruel and ugly. That is why people have been forced to defend their prejudice. And that is why their defenses have been pretty strange!

In the nineteenth century, for example, many people tried to use a religious excuse to cover their prejudice. They said that slavery was a way of introducing the Christian religion to the Africans, who had their own, different religion. It was obvious to the majority of people that this was not a very good excuse, and so some people tried to find a better one. These people turned to the idea that some people were born better than others — smarter, nicer-looking, with better manners, and more honest.

Today we know that this is completely untrue. Today we know that, any way you look at it, there is no excuse good enough to defend prejudice.

Nine out of ten times when a person hears the word
"ghetto" they think of Black people first of all.
They think just about every Black child comes from
a Ghetto with lots of brothers and sisters.
Ghetto has become a definition meaning Black,
garbage, slum areas. To me the word "ghetto" is
just as bad as cursing. I think they put all Black
people in a box marked "ghetto" which leaves them
having no identity. They should let Black people
be seen for themselves, not as one reflection on all.
Vanessa Howard, Age 14

3

PREJUDICE: HOW IT FEELS

"One Man Is No More Than Another
If He Does No More Than Another"
Miguel De Cervantes

It is easy to define what prejudice is. It is also easy to discuss why prejudice occurs. It is much more difficult to describe how it affects people. But of one thing we may be sure: prejudice hurts everyone. Prejudice hurts both the people it is directed against and the people who themselves are prejudiced.

Prejudice hurts other people in a number of ways. First, and most important, it doesn't allow individuals the right to think and act for themselves. It limits their ability to keep growing and learning. Often the victim of prejudice doesn't have the educational, social, and economic opportunities that are the right of every citizen under the law in this country. This sets apart the victims of prejudice from the rest of society by pushing them into different neighborhoods, clubs, and groups.

SEPARATION OF GROUPS | The sit-ins and the freedom rides that occurred in the late 1950's and early 1960's were a response to this kind of separation. At that time there were separate lunch counters for blacks and whites, separate waiting rooms, even separate doorways. Many courts also used separate Bibles. When black people wanted to travel somewhere, even to go to work, they were forced to sit in the rear of the bus or in separate cars on trains. In 1955, Mrs. Rosa Parks, a middle-aged black woman, was returning from work one evening in Montgomery, Alabama. She got on a city bus, paid her fare, and walked past the section reserved for whites. She sat in the first seat of the "blacks only" section. As the bus went on and made its many stops, it became crowded. Finally there were no more seats in the white section. The bus driver ordered the blacks to give up their seats to some white men who had just gotten on the bus. Mrs. Parks refused and she was arrested immediately. To protest the arrest of Mrs. Parks, and to protest the practice of unequal rights for blacks, the Rev. Martin Luther King, Jr. organized a strike against the entire city bus system. After the bus company had lost a great deal of money, and after the Supreme Court ruled it illegal to force blacks to sit separately, the bus company gave in and allowed the blacks to sit anywhere they wanted to on the bus.

The sit-in became popular early in 1960. In sit-ins, blacks and whites who wanted to help would sit at lunch counters where blacks had not been allowed and ask to be served. If they were refused, they would remain seated. These people faced arrests, fines, mob action, and loss of jobs. But they were non-violent. They refused to give up and slowly their action brought about some change.

For more than a hundred years blacks had been made to feel inferior because they were treated as if they were not as good as whites. A more recent example of how prejudice can be harmful in this way was found in the New York City schools, where many of the students are children of Puerto Rican immigrants. Until just a short time ago, these children, who had only a very limited knowledge of the English language, were always tested in the English language. Because they knew and understood only basic English, they were, for the most part, labeled "dull students" and placed in slow classes. Naturally they were aware of their low standing and they lost their desire to learn and to do well in school. Some were often absent from class, and others came but never seemed prepared. It became a common belief among many other students as well as some teachers that Puerto Rican students were "stupid."

But an interesting thing happened when some teachers got together and decided to test these students in their own language. They discovered that these students who were labeled "dull" were, when tested in Spanish, really quite bright. School programs run in both Spanish and English were tried as an experiment. The success of the programs was amazing. The students did much better in their school work and were more interested in learning. In one class the math score of each pupil

doubled, and in others the reading levels of the students rose by at least two or three years. When the students were asked what was responsible for the change in their behavior, they explained that they were free to be themselves since they were no longer being treated as if they were "stupid" or "dull" and not as good as other students. Programs in English and Spanish are now being used in many of the cities with large numbers of Spanish-speaking people.

THE VICTIM | The victims of prejudice are often, like these Puerto Rican students, made fun of, treated cruelly, and insulted. They are very often not included in the opportunities and the privileges that most of us enjoy. Always being on the "outside," always being left out of experiences that others take for granted, and always being told that you are somehow "not quite good enough" finally leaves you with a pretty bad view of yourself. This is the saddest effect of prejudice. The victim of prejudice, unable to break through the fences that separate him from the rest of society, begins to lose confidence in himself and in his abilities. He begins to "give up."

When someone tells you often enough that you can't do something, you begin to believe that you can't do it. You give up trying to find out what you are capable of.

The person who is prejudiced is also his own victim. He damages himself as well as other people. He hides his fears, his failures, and his shortcomings behind his prejudice. He is basically a person who is unhappy with himself. In order to make himself feel better, he finds a target for the anger and bad feeling that he has toward himself. This is certainly a very common experience. Which one of us has not become angry with a sister, a brother, or a friend (especially if they are younger) when we are really angry with ourselves?

The prejudiced person is afraid to be "different." He wants very much to "fit in," to belong, to be accepted. The prejudiced person accepts without question the thoughts and values of the majority and of the group that he wants to belong to. Sadly, he never struggles to find out what it is that is special about himself. He never expresses *who* he is.

HOW DOES PREJUDICE FEEL? | Recently a fourth-grade teacher decided that she wanted her students to really understand how prejudice works and how it feels. These students had heard a great deal about prejudice, but none of them had ever experienced it. They lived in a small town in Iowa. Most of the people in their town looked pretty much alike, had the same background, and seemed to share most of the same values and goals. Their problem was to find or create a situation in which they would be able to experience the effects of prejudice. Their teacher, Jane Elliot, helped them by pointing out that one difference among them was eye color. People had for years been treated unfairly because of their skin color, type of hair, and religion, so why not use eye color? The students agreed, and so they were separated into a blue-eyed group and a brown-eyed group.

Since the teacher was blue-eyed, she decided that on the first day of the experiment the blue-eyed students would be better, and on the next day they would change roles and the brown-eyed students would be better. This way both groups had the chance to experience what it felt like to be "superior" and "inferior."

The class felt at first that the experiment would be fun. They laughed together and looked forward to the first day of the experiment. On the first day, all the blue-eyed students were allowed to sit in the front of the room, while the brown-eyed students were forced to sit in the back. To make sure that the brown-eyed students stayed in their place and didn't pretend to be blue-eyed, they had to wear collars around their necks. As the class began, the blue-eyed teacher started calling on the brown-eyed students and making fun of them when they didn't know the right answers. Soon the brown-eyed students became very nervous when the teacher called on them. They were afraid that she would make fun of them in front of the whole class. They began to mumble their answers and forget information they had known very clearly only that morning. At recess time, only the blue-eyed students were allowed to use the playground. The brown-eyed students had to stay inside. The teacher also gave the blue-eyed students five extra minutes of play. At lunch, the brown-eyed students had to wait behind the blue-eyed students in the line. The teacher told them they couldn't have seconds, but the blue-eyed students could have extras if they wanted.

By afternoon, it was clear that experimenting with prejudice was no fun at all.

During the lunch period, the blue-eyed students started calling the brown-eyed students "brownies." They made fun of the "brownies" by calling them lazy, stupid, and dirty. The brown-eyed students were angry, but they were hurt, too. It was hard to believe that only yesterday they had all been friends. The brown-eyed students started to fight back. Several students were involved in fistfights and shoving matches.

When the students went back to the classroom after lunch, things did not improve. The teacher was very angry with the brown-eyed students for fighting. She made fun of them again in front of the whole class. When they began doing their schoolwork, it became clear to everybody that the brown-eyed students couldn't keep up with the blue-eyed students. This was very strange because before the experiment with prejudice the entire class was able to work at just about the same level. The brown-eyed students were really unhappy now, and the blue-eyed students really felt that they were better. The fighting and anger between the two groups continued for the rest of the afternoon.

Everybody was happy when the day was over — the teacher, the brown-eyed group, and even the blue-eyed group.

Members of the blue-eyed group were happy during the beginning of the experiment. One boy said that he was happy because he felt like a king and that he was "ruling" over the brown-eyed people. Generally the blue-eyed people felt happy because they felt that they were superior. They liked getting all the special attention, they liked feeling smarter and better than the other students. Yet when they bullied the "brownies" and called them names, they felt mean and nasty. After a while they began to miss their friends in the brown-eyed group. Finally they just felt unhappy and lonely.

The brown-eyed people felt terrible throughout the whole experiment. They realized from the beginning when Mrs. Elliot put the collars around their necks to prevent them from passing for "bluies" that they weren't going to get any fun out of the experiment at all. At first they tried to protect themselves by arguing whenever Mrs. Elliot or one of the "bluies" said something bad about brown-eyed people. But nobody paid any attention to them. And so they just accepted all the bad comments after a while. It seemed to the "brownies" that their teacher and the rest of the class had simply stopped looking at them. They were the same boys and girls they had been the day before, but nobody in the class seemed to care about that after they started wearing their collars. All of the "brownies" felt completely left out and they were hurt, unhappy, and angry. They also felt helpless, since no matter what they did the "bluies" treated them the same way. Finally, one by one, they just "gave up" and went along with the situation. This made them feel even worse and they began to hate themselves for not fighting back. There just didn't seem to be any way out of the problem.

On the second day of the experiment, the rules were switched — the brown-eyed students became "superior" and the blue-eyed students became "inferior." The same thing happened.

The teacher found the whole experiment very educational and yet frightening at the same time. She thought it was educational because she learned that victims of prejudice did indeed become "dumb" when they were treated as if they were "dumb." She saw bright students, who the day before had done very well in math and spelling, fail math and spelling tests. She saw students, who knew their studies very well, suddenly lose confidence in themselves and become frightened of being called on.

She was frightened because she saw students, who had always been cooperative and well-mannered, suddenly change overnight and become mean little bullies. She felt the experiment proved that all of us are capable of prejudiced behavior, and that frightened her very much.

Another experiment was performed with teachers. In this experiment, two teachers were given classes to teach. Both classes were at the same level of progress and the students in each of these classes had received the same kinds of grades.

But the teachers were told that one class was stupid and one class was smart.

Then they began to teach their separate classes.

After some time they were asked to report on the progress of their classes. The teacher who thought she had a smart class reported that her class was doing good work, and that the students were performing well.

The teacher who thought her class was stupid reported that her students were slow. She said they were unable to keep up with their work, they had trouble answering questions in class, and, in general, they were poor students.

Both of these classes were tested when the experiment was over. The class that was labeled "smart" had stayed at exactly the same level as before the experiment began, but the class that was labeled "slow" had really become slow. In some cases the individual I.Q. test levels of students had actually dropped.

What had happened was that the teacher who thought her

class was smart treated her students as if they were smart. The teacher who thought her class was slow treated her students as if they were stupid.

The conclusion of the experimenters was exactly the same conclusion that Mrs. Elliot and her class came to: when you are treated in an unfair way, you begin to feel and even act as if you are not as good as other people.

PREJUDICE HURTS EVERYONE | The experience of practicing and feeling prejudice shows very clearly that prejudice is a two-way street: it twists the prejudiced person as well as the victim. These experiments prove that prejudice not only hurts, but really changes the way you act, the way you think about yourself, and the way you do your work.

When these experiments were over, the students who took part in them had new answers to many questions, questions like these:

If you knew that no matter how hard you worked you would be called "dumb," would that make you try your hardest and do your best work?

If being treated unfairly in school made you feel angry or left out, would you want to go to school?

What would you feel like if you were told, over and over again, that you were "bad," "dirty," or "lazy"?

Is it any better to judge a person by the color of his skin or by his religion than by the color of his eyes?

These experiments were a very hard way to find out about prejudice. Yet all these students learned a great deal about themselves and about people in general.

They learned that we must never be afraid to look at ourselves and at each other. They learned that we must always try to see ourselves and others as we really are. And most important, they learned that only in this way can we really be free.

4

PREJUDICE: THEN AND NOW

"These are some of the nationalities of the world.
They all speak many languages.
Everyone has their own language
which they speak and understand.
Everyone is different and alike in many ways.
Everyone has a different religion.
But everyone is equal."
A Fifth Grader

When we look back in time, we begin to understand why prejudice today is such a difficult problem. Just a quick review of our history shows that prejudice has grown in our country as America itself grew from its original thirteen colonies.

PREJUDICE THEN | Our country was settled in the seventeenth and eighteenth centuries by people from every country in Europe. Most of these people came to the new world to escape prejudice and unfair treatment. In their own countries they had suffered a great deal because, in some ways, they were different from other people. In most cases they were different from other people simply because they had different religious beliefs. They all saw America as a place where they would be able to worship in any way they wanted. They thought that America would offer them the freedom to express their beliefs and to really be themselves. Curiously, however, these people were themselves guilty of prejudice, and were cruel to people who had religions or beliefs different from their own.

Even the colonial period of our history was a time of great strife. At first there was little cooperation between the thirteen colonies because of the distrust and suspicion they felt for one another. Our forefathers forgot all the things they had in common because they could only see their religious differences.

The Puritans of Massachusetts, for example, had suffered great hardships in England where they were treated cruelly because of their beliefs. But when they settled in Massachusetts, they themselves would not allow anyone to disagree with their beliefs.

The Puritans would not accept the Quakers. There were many laws against allowing Quakers into the colony of Massachusetts. If a Quaker was found in the colony, he lost an ear. If he was discovered a second time, he lost his other ear. If he was found a third time, his tongue was burnt with a red-hot iron. Yet the Quakers took pride in their faith and it was important to them that they not seem afraid of the Puritans. So they often came to Massachusetts and there was a great deal of fighting. At one time it was a common sight to see Quakers hanging in Boston Common.

The famous Salem Witch Trials of the 1690s are another example of the kind of prejudice that the Puritans practiced. Many people during this period in our history believed in the evil power of witches. In Salem, Massachusetts, in 1692 there was a general panic, and all those who seemed somehow "different" were accused of witchcraft. Nineteen were hanged.

Not all of the colonists were as prejudiced as the Puritans, but they were prejudiced in less bloody ways. The colony of Virginia, for example, threw out all Puritan ministers and threatened that if they did not leave, they would be killed. Maryland in 1649 passed an act which granted freedom of worship to all who believed in Jesus Christ, but provided for the death of all who denied Jesus' divinity. Truly, at the birth of our nation, prejudice was as ugly and as widespread as it is today.

Yet the leaders of our country during the colonial period were able to see the dangers of a society that was torn from within by prejudice. In the Declaration of Independence and the Bill of Rights, they set forth the principles of equality and freedom for all men.

Unfortunately, although we in America have tried, we have not always lived up to the goals that were set down by our forefathers.

We have only to look at the fairly recent past of slavery and the Civil War to realize that we have always had to struggle to fulfill the promise of our country. The Civil War did not bring an end to the evils of slavery, and even during the Civil War the 200,000 blacks who served in the Union army and navy were not accepted happily. Twenty-two of these black men won the Medal of Honor, and yet all the black units received second-rate training, weapons, and medical care. For eighteen months the blacks were granted only one-half of the pay of the white soldiers.

After the Civil War, the leaders of our country tried very hard to soothe the prejudice of the North against the South and the South against the North. Today, over one hundred years later, we have had some success, but we must still keep trying.

The Civil War did not really free blacks. Almost as soon as the war was over, laws separating blacks from whites sprang up all over the country, and especially in the South. In many states blacks and whites were not even allowed to mix in places of worship! Unjust treatment of blacks was just as bad in the North as it was in the South. A law was passed in Pennsylvania taking away the free blacks' right to vote. The same thing happened in many other Northern states.

During the nineteenth and twentieth centuries, waves of immigrants came to seek the promise of America. Each of the groups that arrived — the Irish, the Jews, the Italians, and recently, people from Cuba and Puerto Rico — were met with prejudice. The faces of the people in our ghettos have changed over the years. But the ghettos themselves remain.

Gradually, the people of America became aware of the dangers of prejudice. Gradually, they have come to see that it is prejudice that threatens our country more than almost anything else.

During World War II, half a million blacks fought in units that were separated from whites. When Charles Drew, a black doctor, developed the blood bank system in 1941, the Red Cross kept separate "white" and "black" blood banks. The inequality of this situation was not changed until 1948 when President Truman ordered that all units in the armed forces must be mixed. President Truman acted because he saw the stupidity of armed forces fighting for liberty and freedom while not giving liberty and freedom to a large portion of their own soldiers.

PREJUDICE NOW | We have come to understand that a society tends to break down when the rules that govern that society are different for different groups. In order for society to run smoothly, there must be some specific general ways of behaving that are accepted by all the members of that society. No one should have special privileges or opportunities. No group should be punished because it is different.

Unfortunately, however, people's attitudes don't change very

quickly. Although we have come to understand the dangers of prejudice, we are still far from solving the problem of prejudice. Today there are still many people being treated unfairly because they are "different."

Groups that have been treated unfairly have become impatient over the years. They have waited a long time for these slow changes to affect their lives and the way they are treated. More and more, these groups are challenging unfair treatment and bringing their feelings to the attention of the public.

PREJUDICE IN A DEMOCRACY | Prejudice is a threat to democratic life. If we deny the dignity of an individual, if we put a collar around his or her neck, we are going against the basic principles of the democratic way of life. Equality in America means giving everybody equal opportunity to get the kind of education they want, to live in the neighborhood they want, and to be able to get the kind of job they want. Prejudice denies people equal opportunity. If our nation is to grow, if it is to fulfill the promise it has held forth for two hundred years, we must prove once and for all that some people are not born "more equal" than others.

For many years, America had no laws of any kind to prevent people from acting upon their hatred for other people. Before the Civil War, the law permitted slaves to be viewed not as people, but as pieces of property or as animals. Slave-owners could buy or sell slaves, mistreat them, or even kill them. During the earlier part of this century hotels and restaurants had signs saying "No Jews Allowed" or "No Irish Allowed". There was nothing in the law to stop these practices.

During the nineteenth and the early part of the twentieth centuries, there was no way to stop cartoons in newspapers and magazines that made fun of and insulted the minority people who came to this country looking for a new home. It was not

47

illegal to separate black children, Mexican American children, or American Indian children from white children and to put them in different schools. It was not illegal for one person to refuse to hire another because of his color or his religion.

Within the past few years, however, we have tried to protect the dignity and worth of all human beings by law. Today it is illegal to practice prejudice in the ways mentioned above. In 1954, the Supreme Court ruled that separation due to color, race, or religion was illegal; it ordered all schools in this country to provide equal and mixed education for all students.

People themselves were busy during this period. This was the time of the sit-in demonstrations that we spoke of before. It was a time when individuals of different religions, backgrounds, and colors came together to end the separation of blacks and whites. It was also the time of the "Freedom Riders," and of people like Rosa Parks who brought the unfairness of separation on buses, trains, and planes to the attention of the public. Hundreds and hundreds of people — students, housewives, doctors, saleswomen, lawyers, clergymen of all religions, construction workers, and secretaries — worked together to make people everywhere realize that all people should be treated in the same way. They worked to change people's minds and they worked to change the law.

Finally in 1964, the Congress of the United States signed into law the Civil Rights Act which does not allow any individual to be treated unfairly because of race, creed, or color. Today, we have many laws that make unfair treatment based on "differentness" illegal. But the struggle still goes on. Although it's difficult to change laws, it's even more difficult to change people's beliefs and attitudes. There are many disagreements in both the North and the South about bussing, for example. And some people are still denied equal opportunity because of race, religion, and sex.

PREJUDICE AND THE LAW | Laws can state that the practice of prejudice is illegal, but laws alone cannot stop people from being prejudiced.

As long as people continue to hate and fear others whom they regard as "different," they will continue to show their prejudice in underhanded and sneaky ways. Prejudiced people may not break the law, but often they will bend it.

For instance, suppose a black family wants to move into a neighborhood where everyone else is white. The white people can't directly refuse to let the black family move in. But they can threaten the white family that sells the house, or the real estate broker who shows the black family homes for sale in a "white neighborhood." And if the black family manages to move into the neighborhood in spite of all these obstacles, the people in their neighborhood can make life very hard for them. For example, in 1957, a black family moved into a white community in Levittown, New York. This community had always been all white. William Myers, Jr., his wife, and their three children were the first blacks. Every night angry crowds of as many as five hundred people gathered near their home. One night some people in the crowd threw stones that broke the living room windows. Over and over, there were bloody clashes between state troopers and angry white residents. Mr. and Mrs. Myers, who had worked hard and saved carefully for their new home, were hurt and angry. Their three young children who were kept locked in their home were frightened. The problem was that most of the people who lived in Levittown then really didn't care what kind of people the Myers were. They looked only at the color of their skin and saw the Myers as "blacks," not as people. The prejudice that the Myers family faced was out in the open, but underhanded prejudice can hurt just as much.

Here's an example of underhanded prejudice. Suppose a Mexican boy, Pedro, studies very hard to get a good education.

Pedro lives in a poor neighborhood and he goes to a school that is old and overcrowded. Some of his teachers feel that he is too "dumb" or "bad" to learn. But Pedro studies hard, goes to his special tutoring class, and gets a good education in spite of his bad school. Pedro applies for a job. His employer cannot, under the law, refuse him a job if he has all the necessary skills. But if the employer is prejudiced against Mexicans, he can still find ways to avoid hiring Pedro. He can make everyone applying for the job take a test that includes questions on subjects taught only in the white schools in town. There are many ways to bend the law.

MINORITY AMERICANS | Minority people, called minority because they have a "different" skin color, religion, nationality, or race from most Americans, have a very hard time breaking the circle of prejudice that closes around their lives. Refused homes in "white neighborhoods," they live in the worst housing in the country. In big cities, they are crowded together in ghettos, which are in the oldest and dirtiest neighborhoods. Often they cannot move from the ghettos because they are too poor to afford better apartments or homes. They are too poor because they cannot get jobs that will pay well. And they can't get well-paying jobs because they are poorly educated.

Minority people did not create the conditions — ghettos, poor schools, low-paying jobs — that keep them down and out, but "majority" people often blame minority people for their problems and poor conditions. They refuse to see the people as victims. They say that if minority people live in ghettos, it is because they are "not as good," or because they really don't want to "help themselves." When "majority" people say things like this, they are really saying, "I am not responsible," "It isn't my fault, I just mind my own business."

Prejudice can still be seen everywhere in our society. We find it in books and movies and magazines and on television. Often the very textbooks we use in school show minority people as somehow not as good.

Take, for example, the way American Indians have been described until recently. In most history books, the story of Custer's Last Stand shows the Indians as mindless savages, while only the white soldiers are shown as capable of bravery and honor. The Indians in reality were protecting their land and their way of life. In their actions they were both brave and honorable.

Until recently in TV commercials and in films, Spanish-speaking people were shown wearing big floppy hats and sleeping in the sun. This picture implied they never did any work and were lazy. In fact, many Spanish-speaking cultures have a rest or *siesta* during the heat of midday.

Women are not a minority group in terms of numbers, but they, too, are victims of prejudice. Advertisements often seem to say that women are nothing but pretty, empty things, and textbooks hardly mention their achievements at all. Although 40% of all women work fulltime because they must help support their families, they usually make less money than men for the same work.

Movies, television, magazines, and textbooks are not as prejudiced against minorities as they once were. Today, we see people from many different minority groups in major television shows and commercials. Textbooks now also include information about minority people.

Nevertheless, studies tell us that we have a long way to go. In spite of the fact that most of the poor in this country are white (because the majority of the total population is white), a non-white's chance of being poor is one in eight. A Spanish-speaking person's odds are one in three, while for blacks, the odds are one in two or fifty-fifty.

The unfair treatment and poor living conditions that are the result of prejudice make minority people strangers in their own country, just as the students in Mrs. Elliot's class felt like strangers in their own classroom when they became targets of prejudice. Prejudice keeps minority people from having a chance to get the things that everybody wants — a decent home, a job, education, and the right to be viewed as an individual person instead of as a member of a group.

5

WHAT YOU CAN DO

"They are all people.
Some are good and some are not.
Just because they are another
race or religion does not
make a lower class of life.
Everyone is equal."
A Seventh Grader

Prejudice doesn't have to happen. We are not born prejudiced, you remember. We learn to hate. Surely we can unlearn, too.

Surprising as it may seem, it is easy for human beings to get used to change. It is even easy for prejudiced people to get used to change. In Panama, for example, there are places where one side of the street is in the American Canal Zone, and the other side of the street is in Panama. Something very curious happened to the blacks and whites living in this area. On the American Zone side, blacks were treated unfairly. On the Panama side, blacks received equal treatment. When blacks from the Panama side crossed over to the American Zone side, they went along with the unfair treatment even though they were used to living equally with whites where they came from. On the other hand, whites from the American Zone side who went to the Panama side adjusted to treating blacks equally even though they did not treat them equally on the American Zone side. Clearly we are able to change and unlearn attitudes depending on where we live and what the written and unwritten rules are.

But unlearning is not so simple as, say, forgetting all the arithmetic you learned last week. Fighting and overcoming your prejudices requires a lot of effort. We will have to change our attitudes about a lot of things. We will have to learn to look at the world in different ways. We will have to look at ourselves and our actions more closely.

All of us — of every color, religion, and race — need each other. That is the real reason to fight prejudice. We need each other if we are to live free of war. We need each other if we want to build a better world. Most of all, each of us needs each other to be a whole human being.

When we use prejudice, we are really building walls around ourselves to keep other people out. We put labels on people as if they were things. Every time one of us does that, he is reducing the number of friends and experiences he could have.

LONG LIVE DIFFERENCES | The French say, "Vive la différence." That means, "Long live differences." Differences are wonderful. They are what make life interesting. We should all look forward to different people as exciting, new friends.

A lot of harm done to Indians by the white man happened because of the white man's desire to change the Indians into people more like himself. The early Indian reformers really believed that the best thing for the red man was for him to learn to be like his white brother. This led to such acts as the Dawes Act of 1887 which broke down the old tribal structures and divided a number of Indian reservations into 160-acre lots similar to those formed by the white settlers. Since the Indians had little skill or interest in white man's farming and had no idea of private ownership, this system made no sense. Indian reformers wanted to help the Indians, but they wanted to help them only to be like whites. They were unable to accept the fact that Indians and whites led different kinds of lives.

America was born as a country especially for all the varied peoples of the world. This land began as a "melting pot." Recently, however, the idea of America as a "melting pot" began to change. People discovered that they really didn't want to give up their differences and their own, special identities. Today, most people want America to become a place where all the different groups keep their separate identities, but live together in peace and brotherhood. The American poet Walt Whitman put it this way: "America is not merely a nation, but a teeming nation of nations."

The whole world is watching, says author James Baldwin, to see if we can "achieve America."

The Declaration of Independence, for example, clearly states,

"All men are created equal." All men, says the Declaration, have rights which cannot be taken away from them. Among these rights are life, liberty, and the pursuit of happiness. They are for everybody, not a special few.

The Bill of Rights is another document of democracy. It grants people freedoms like freedom of speech, religion, and assembly. It applies to everyone. We do not have one set of freedoms for the rich and one for the poor, one set for white people and another for black people. We are all promised equal rights. That is our ideal.

Two shipwrecked men were washed up on a deserted shore. When they had rested a little and were able to walk, they explored the land eagerly, only to discover that it was round, for it was an island. Then they were heavy at heart. The wind blew, rain fell upon them, and at night the island was cold.

Hurriedly they set to work building houses, each for himself. But it was hard, because one man could scarcely lift a beam alone.

When they searched for food for their stomachs, they worked hard again, for there was not enough. They grabbed whatever they could find and stuffed it into their mouths. One even seized some tiny fish out of a stream and ate them raw. The other cried out at him, "You are a savage!"

The first grew very angry but said nothing.

When at last they had time to look about a little, they found they both were poor, having nothing but the work of their hands. The second man tried to make himself feel less ragged. He gathered gay-colored birds' feathers from the beach and tied them round his head, thinking they made him handsome.

"You fool!" cried the first, showing at last how angry he was. "Look at you! What a fool you are!"

"I will not be called fool by a savage!" shouted the second.

Each rushed to the other's house and tore it down.

And they were heavy at heart, for the wind blew, rain fell upon them, and at night the island was cold.

Gradually their tempers cooled.

At last one set to work again to build himself a house, while the other stood watching. It was hard, because one man could scarcely lift a beam into place alone.

Then he called out, "Come help me! And I will help you build yours."

So they worked together. And it was easier. Soon they both had better houses than before.

"Let us always stand ready to help each other," said one. "Life will be better this way on our island. And you may eat your fish any way you want to. That is nothing to me."

"Very well," agreed the other. "And I will not think you are a fool no matter what you wear. If we are to be friends, we must accept one another."

Those two men are you and me, and the island is round because it is the world. And too many of us are poor, without enough food to eat or good clothes to wear. Fearing people who are different, each of us has been squandering his money on bombs with which to destroy the others.

Life can be better on our round island if we help one another to build houses. We cannot afford to go on tearing down what little we have. Tom Galt

PREJUDICE AND YOU | What can *you* do about prejudice?

Start with a long, hard look at yourself. Are you prejudiced? Be honest. Against whom? Why? You have to be aware of your own feelings before you can start to change.

Think back to unkind remarks you might have made about groups of people. Nearly all of us have made such prejudiced remarks. What caused them? Was there an experience or incident in your background that made you have certain opinions about different kinds of people? Did you jump too quickly to a conclusion? Were you being unfair?

Think about the way you look at people. Do you label them? "Italians are dirty," "women are emotional," "policemen are mean," or "construction workers are stupid," for example? If so, why? Are these judgments you heard once and believed? Are your prejudices based simply on not knowing better? Are you looking for a scapegoat?

Even though you may say that you do not believe, for instance, that "construction workers are stupid," do you treat all construction workers as if they were? That is prejudice, too, you know.

To fight your prejudices, the first step is to get to know people. And the best way to get to know them is to learn about them, to meet them. How much do you know about the people you make fun of? How many different kinds of people can you count among your friends? Do you live and go to school and play only with people just like you?

Here are some things all of us can do to break out of our narrow world.

1. Read. How much do you know about black history, Spanish-American history, American Indian history? How much do you know about the customs and traditions and beliefs of America's religious groups? How about the foods, dress, ceremonies, language, and expressions of Americans of Chinese, Japanese, Polish, German, French, Italian, and Irish descent? For that matter, how much do you know about the ways of life found in America's South, West, Midwest, or Atlantic seaboard?

You can find these answers in history books, novels about people from different countries, and works by black and other minority authors. Also read the newspapers and magazines written for groups other than your own.

2. View. Try to watch television news shows and programs about the lives of Americans from different countries and racial backgrounds and about the problems of prejudice due to race and religion.

3. Walk in others' shoes. Read the life stories of famous Americans from different backgrounds to understand the way that victims of prejudice view the outside world.

4. Search out friends of different races and national backgrounds. See if you can join a Girl Scout or Boy Scout troop, a girls' club or boys' club that includes many different kinds of people. Join an all-city sports team or music club. Invite your new friends to your home.

5. Talk to your family and friends about their feelings toward "different" people. Speak out against prejudiced remarks and attitudes.

6. Always view people for their individual worth, not the groups to which they belong.

All these actions will help you change your attitude and maybe the attitudes of the people that you know. Yet they are only part of the answer to the problem of prejudice.

Another part of the solution is the laws that have been passed to make it illegal to act out prejudice through unfair treatment. It is important that these laws be respected and enforced.

Slowly, America has changed some of the injustices of prejudice. Slowly, the American people have become aware of the damage that prejudice can do to our society. Yet, in spite of all the changes that have occurred during the past few years, we have a long way to go. Examples of unfair treatment are still everywhere in our society. We read about them in our newspapers and we see them reported on television. Fighting prejudice — America's worst problem — and overcoming the hate that divides people will require all the love and wisdom and courage that we have.

But the fight is worth it.

SELECTED
BIBLIOGRAPHY

SOURCE MATERIAL

Allport, Gordon W. *ABC's of Scapegoating.* New York City: Anti-Defamation League of B'nai B'rith, 1948, revised edition 1959. Analyzes the motives, sources, and forms of scapegoating and race prejudice.

Courlander, Harold. *On Recognizing the Human Species.* New York City: Anti-Defamation League of B'nai B'rith, 1960. Shows that superficial social differences cannot disguise the basic similarities of man's traditions and customs all over the world.

Goodman, Mary Ellen. *Race Awareness in Young Children.* New York City: Collier Books, 1964. Discusses the impact of race awareness on the behavior of young children.

Lee, Irving J. *How Do You Talk About People.* New York City: Anti-Defamation League of B'nai B'rith, 1954. A practical guide to clear thinking and accurate communication, by the late president of the International Society of General Semantics.

Montagu, Ashley. *What We Know About Race.* New York City: Anti-Defamation League of B'nai B'rith, 1958. Examines the beginnings of man, his adaptive traits, environment and intelligence, and points out that scientists have not yet reached a single acceptable definition of "race."

Rose, Peter I. *They and We: Racial & Ethnic Relations in the United States.* New York City: Random House, 1964. A review of some of the principal aspects of racial and ethnic relations in the United States.

Spock, Dr. Benjamin. *Prejudice in Children: A Conversation with Dr. Benjamin Spock.* New York City: Anti-Defamation League of B'nai B'rith, 1963. The eminent pediatrician and writer on baby and child care debunks the shibboleths of "hereditary" prejudice.

Tumin, Melvin M., ed. *Race and Intelligence.* New York City: Anti-Defamation League of B'nai B'rith, 1963. Four distinguished social scientists examine in detail the charge that blacks have a lower native intelligence than whites. The four agree that scientific evidence indicates race has no relationship to intelligence.

Van Til, William. *Prejudiced: How Do People Get That Way?* New York City: Anti-Defamation League of B'nai B'rith, 1957. Cogent explanation of how people become prejudiced and how prejudice can be prevented.

The above titles published by the Anti-Defamation League of B'nai B'rith are available at 315 Lexington Avenue, New York, New York 10016, and regional offices throughout the country.

SUGGESTIONS FOR RELATED READINGS

Beim, Lorraine. *Carol's Side of the Street.* New York City: Harcourt Brace Jovanovich, Inc., 1951.

Johnston, Johanna. *Together in America: The Story of Two Races and One Nation.* New York City: Dodd, 1965.

Peterson, Edward and Barbara N. *Case of the Door-Openers Vs. the Fence Builders.* New York City: Friendship Press, 1967.

ABOUT
THE AUTHORS

Irene Fandel Gersten was born in New York City. After graduating from Queens College, Ms. Gersten did graduate work in English at the State University of New York at Binghamton, where she subsequently served as a member of the faculty. Ms. Gersten has taught courses in Western literature, from the Greek and Roman Classics to the twentieth century novel. After leaving Binghamton, Ms. Gersten worked in textbook publishing and is presently an editor and writer at the Anti-Defamation League of B'nai B'rith. Ms. Gersten, who is married and lives in New York City, is now working on a book about stereotypes in American fiction of the 1920s and 30s.

Betsy Bliss is a free lance writer with special interests in education and human relations. Ms. Bliss received a Masters Degree from the Medill School of Journalism at Northwestern University. She has taught school and served as a reporter for the *Chicago Daily News*. Ms. Bliss has also been a staff-member of the New York State Commission on Equality, Cost and Financing of Elementary Education (the Fleischmann Commission). Ms. Bliss lives in New York City.

ABOUT
THE ILLUSTRATOR

Richard Rosenblum is a successfull free lance illustrator. A graduate of Cooper Union College, he lives in Brooklyn, New York with his wife and daughter. His work has appeared in many books and magazines.

ABOUT THE ANTI-DEFAMATION LEAGUE OF B'NAI B'RITH

For sixty active years the Anti-Defamation League of B'nai B'rith has served as an educating force in American life. Anti-Defamation League programs have been directed, in particular, to combating discrimination against minorities, to fighting the threat of all forms of totalitarianism, and to promoting understanding and cooperation among all the religious faiths in America.